EVERYTHING
VOLCANOES & EARTHQUAKES

NATIONAL GEOGRAPHIC KiDS

EVERYTHING VOLCANOES & EARTHQUAKES

BY KATHY FURGANG

With National Geographic Explorer CARSTEN PETER

CONTENTS

Lava flows into the ocean at Kaula-Kona, Hawaii, U.S.A., at sunrise.

The lava from Ol Doinyo Lengai volcano in Tanzania can harden in midair and then shatter like glass.

INTRODUCTION

PLANET EARTH IS FULL OF
ACTION. ON ANY GIVEN DAY, EARTHQUAKES
shake the ground and split the surface with deep gashes.
Volcanic mountains spew rock and thick ash into the air.
Fiery-hot rivers of lava flow, then gradually cool to form
new landmasses. Even the ocean floor changes constantly.
Lava oozes from underwater volcanoes—geologists have
identified more than 5,000 of them! Many of these rise over
time to break the surface and form islands. Then wind and
pounding waves take over, shaping each new landform.

To understand this changing landscape, you have to
go back about 4.5 billion years to when the planet first
formed. No time machine? Then, stay right here and hang
on for a wild ride as we scale the slopes of an active volcano and shake, rattle, and roll with a mighty quake. Let's
discover EVERYTHING about volcanoes and earthquakes!

EXPLORER'S CORNER

Hi! I'm Carsten Peter.

I'm a photographer who loves to take
pictures of places where no one else
can go. My mission takes
me to some of the
scariest places on Earth:
volcanoes, toxic and
superheated caves,
turbulent lava lakes.
These aren't exactly
places where my smart-
phone camera works. So
one of the challenges I
face, especially when I'm
working for National Geographic, is to
create special techniques to capture
the shots I want. So get ready. Just this
once, I'm going to take you with me.

The constant shifting and shaking of Earth's layers builds mountains and moves continents, shaping the surface of the planet. When these natural forces get rough, earthquakes rumble and volcanoes erupt, like Mount Bromo in Indonesia, pictured here.

1

WHEN EARTH CRACKS UP

WHAT IS A VOLCANO?

IT'S SERIOUSLY

HOT 4,000 MILES (6,437 KM) DOWN AT THE CENTER OF THE EARTH.

The temperature there ranges from 9032°F to 12,632°F (5000 to 7000°C) That kind of heat melts rock into liquid, or molten, form. Sometimes molten rock gushes up and bursts through an opening in Earth's surface—a volcano—in a fiery flow of lava. Sometimes a volcano takes the shape of a mountain. Sometimes it even forms underwater.

The Karymsky volcano in Russia is the most active volcano in its region. It's been actively erupting for more than 500 years. The volcano produces a fine, powdered rock called ash, which looks like black smoke.

MAGMA AND LAVA

Magma is molten rock *before* it reaches Earth's surface. Lava is molten rock *after* it reaches the surface. When lava erupts from a volcano, it can be liquid, semiliquid, or solid rock, depending on its temperature. The outer layer of rock can cool within minutes, but thick lava can take years to cool completely.

BUBBLING AND BOILING

Mud pots like these bubble and steam at the base of some volcanic mountains.

Earthquakes can cause changes—and sometimes tremendous damage—on Earth's surface. Earthquakes can rip apart bridges, roads, and buildings (left).

WHAT IS AN EARTHQUAKE?

THE EARTH'S OUTER CRUST MIGHT SEEM ROCK SOLID, BUT IN FACT IT'S PRETTY thin—and put together like a jigsaw puzzle with many natural cracks and breaks. When the crust shifts suddenly we feel things rumbling around. That's an earthquake.

The biggest pieces of the puzzle are called tectonic plates. There are a few major plates and dozens of smaller ones. The edges where the plates touch are called fault lines. When the plates shift along fault lines, magma can rise to the surface and trigger a volcanic eruption. And where the plates pull apart, slide past each other, or crash together, they take what's on the surface for a ground-buckling, earthshaking ride.

Most earthquakes are too small for people to feel them. Every year there may be millions of tiny quakes that go undetected or unnoticed. However, some major earthquakes are so devastating that they cause landslides, fires, collapsed buildings, and even tidal waves thousands of miles away—events that often result in the loss of human lives.

This crack in the ground (above) in Chile, in South America, was caused by aftershocks that rocked the area a month after a big earthquake.

GIANT JIGSAW PUZZLE

Tectonic plates are always on the move. Most action occurs along the edges where two plates meet.

EXPLOSIVE FACT THERE IS A 100 PERCENT CHANCE THAT THERE WILL BE AN EARTHQUAKE SOMEWHERE ON EARTH TODAY!

EARTH BUILDERS

IT'S TIME FOR **YOUR TRIP TO THE CENTER OF EARTH.** That's where all the action you see on the surface starts—thousands of miles below your feet. Think of Earth as a hard-boiled egg. Earth's core is the yolk. Around it, like the white part of the egg, is Earth's thick mantle. And the outer crust, where we live, is like the eggshell. The crust cracks and crumbles when heat from the core heats rock in the mantle. That heating creates currents that push and pull at the plates at the surface. The pushing and pulling results in volcanoes and earthquakes. It can also create some awesome, twisted, beautiful landscapes.

Many volcanoes form at the bottom of the ocean. It takes many thousands of eruptions for these volcanoes to build up and become islands above the surface of the ocean. These volcanic islands sit near the Equator in the Indian Ocean.

EXPLOSIVE FACT HALF OF EARTH'S GEOTHERMAL FEATURES (GEYSERS, FUMAROLES, HOT SPRINGS, AND MUD POTS) ARE IN YELLOWSTONE NATIONAL PARK IN THE U.S.A.

The **CRUST** includes tectonic plates, landmasses, and the ocean. Its thickness varies from 3 to 62 miles (5 to 100 km).

The **MANTLE** is about 1,800 miles (2,897 km) of hot, thick, solid rock.

The **OUTER CORE** is liquid molten lava made mostly of iron and nickel.

The **INNER CORE** is a solid center made mostly of iron and nickel.

Himalaya, India and Tibet

MARVELOUS MOUNTAINS

Earth's plates bump into each other, pushing the surface upward in places. After a few million years, voila—a mountain range!

HEALTHY SOIL Volcanic rock makes soil fertile, which helps trees and food crops grow well.

Volcanoes National Park, Rwanda

GUSHING GEYSERS Geysers are hot springs that erupt, shooting superheated water into the air. Yellowstone National Park in Wyoming and Montana, U.S.A., has more than 300 geysers, including Old Faithful. The famous geyser got its name because it's so predictable: It erupts every 60 to 110 minutes. What's heating up all that water? The park sits on top of a super-volcano—one that could blast out more than a trillion tons of pumice and ash when it erupts. Look out!

VOLCANOES & EARTHQUAKES 13

COLOSSAL QUAKES

THROUGHOUT HISTORY,
VOLCANOES AND EARTHQUAKES HAVE CAUSED GREAT HARDSHIP FOR PEOPLE
all around the world. Even though today's scientists can monitor Earth's movements, they still have no reliable way to predict exactly when a volcano will erupt or an earthquake will strike. That makes preparing for disaster challenging. Earth's tremors and eruptions sometimes catch people by surprise—the result may be a staggering loss of lives and damage to property costing billions of dollars. These are some of the biggest blasts from the past.

QUAKE!

Port-au-Prince, Haiti, 2010
On January 12, 2010, a huge earthquake rocked Port-au-Prince, the capital and largest city of Haiti. The quake killed more than 200,000 people and left some 1.5 million people homeless. The quake also damaged a main port and airport. Dangerous aftershocks rattled the city for months.

QUAKE!

The Call–Chronicle–Examiner

EARTHQUAKE AND FIRE: SAN FRANCISCO IN RUINS

San Francisco, U.S.A., 1906
The 1906 earthquake in San Francisco, California, lasted almost an entire minute, which is a long time when the ground is heaving violently. The earthquake, along with fires that raged for three days, destroyed three-fourths of the city. People as far away as central Nevada—300 miles (483 km) away—felt the shaking.

ERUPTION!

Mount Pelée, Martinique, 1902
A giant volcanic eruption destroyed the village of St. Pierre and killed nearly 30,000 people. In the months after the eruption, thick, sticky lava pushed up from the center of the volcano to form a giant dome. The dome grew fast for a year, sometimes as much as 50 feet (15 m) per day! Finally, the tower collapsed into a pile of rubble.

ERUPTION!

Mount Vesuvius

In A.D. 79, Italy's Mount Vesuvius erupted for 24 straight hours, burying the nearby cities of Pompeii and Herculaneum in ash. Centuries later, archaeologists uncovered the buried cities. They learned that in some places falling ash had piled up as high as nine feet (2.7 m), blocking doorways and crushing roofs.

It's impossible to know how many died, but the remains of about 2,000 people have been found in excavations at Pompeii. The bodies decayed, but ash combined with moisture and molded around them. Scientists poured plaster into some of the solidified ash molds. The resulting plaster casts revealed people clutching jewelry and belongings or hugging each other in their final moments.

Scientists agree that Vesuvius is overdue for another major eruption. Today, one million people live in Naples, Italy, much too close for comfort.

Plaster casts of Pompeii victims

EXPLORER'S CORNER

We know that lots of tiny earthquakes happen every day, and no one even notices. We don't expect to feel a quake unless we live near a major fault line. But sometimes there's a surprise. In the summer of 2011, my colleagues at the Washington, D.C., headquarters of the National Geographic Society were rattled by a 5.8 magnitude quake that sent them running, very confused, from their offices. The quake's epicenter was almost a hundred miles (161 km) away in Virginia! No deaths or serious damage were reported anywhere, but there sure was a lot of texting and tweeting going on.

EXPLOSIVE FACT ARCHAEOLOGISTS FOUND LOAVES OF BREAD STILL SITTING IN AN OVEN IN POMPEII. THE BREAD HAD TURNED TO STONE, PRESERVED IN VOLCANIC ASH!

CHAIN REACTIONS

VOLCANOES AND EARTHQUAKES

LET LOOSE FEARSOME FORCES.

They can cause tremors that set off a chain reaction of movement in water, on land, or in snow.

AVALANCHE

An earthquake can shake a snow-topped mountain—even many miles away from the epicenter. Snowpack gets dislodged and races down slopes in an avalanche, burying whatever is in its path and slamming into the valley below.

The tsunami that followed a massive earthquake in Japan in March 2011 deposited this ship on top of a hotel.

A tsunami is a giant wave that begins beneath the surface of the ocean. It radiates out from an undersea earthquake, landslide, or large volcanic eruption. A tsunami can produce waves 50 to 100 feet (15–30 m) tall that travel at more than 450 miles (724 km) an hour. If one of these towering walls of water reaches land, carrying tons of debris along with it, it can cause massive destruction. Tsunamis lift and toss cars, houses, and even huge ships as if they were toys.

Damage from an aftershock in Christchurch, South Island, New Zealand in 2011

An avalanche races down a 7,000-foot (2,135-m) chute on Pik Kommunizma, Tajikistan.

Heavy rains caused volcanic mudflows on Mount Merapi in Indonesia.

MUDFLOWS

After a volcanic eruption, rivers of mud and debris can spread over wide areas on land. Even months after an eruption, rainwater can combine with the mud and cause further destruction.

AFTERSHOCKS

An earthquake may be strong enough to rattle a town and cause plenty of damage. Afterward, as the ground settles, smaller quakes called aftershocks can occur. These can be just as dangerous as the initial earthquake, causing more severe damage.

EXPLOSIVE FACT THERE ARE ABOUT HALF A MILLION DETECTABLE EARTHQUAKES IN THE WORLD EACH YEAR.

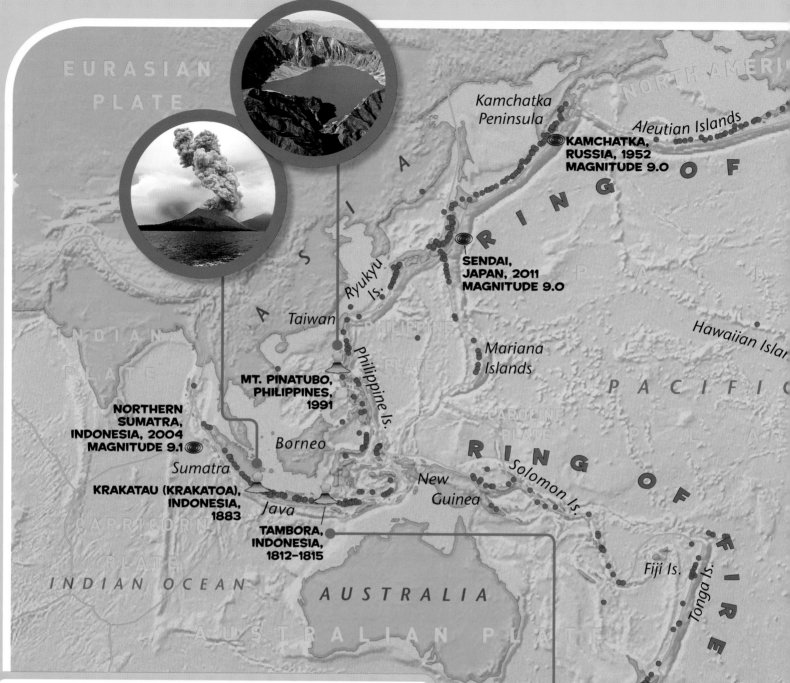

EURASIAN PLATE

Kamchatka Peninsula

Aleutian Islands

NORTH AMERICA

KAMCHATKA, RUSSIA, 1952 MAGNITUDE 9.0

RING OF

SENDAI, JAPAN, 2011 MAGNITUDE 9.0

A S I A

Ryukyu Is.

Taiwan

Mariana Islands

Hawaiian Islands

PACIFIC

MT. PINATUBO, PHILIPPINES, 1991

Philippine Is.

PHILIPPINE PLATE

CAROLINE PLATE

NORTHERN SUMATRA, INDONESIA, 2004 MAGNITUDE 9.1

Borneo

INDIAN PLATE

Sumatra

KRAKATAU (KRAKATOA), INDONESIA, 1883

Java

TAMBORA, INDONESIA, 1812–1815

New Guinea

Solomon Is.

R I N G

O F

F I R E

CAPRICORN PLATE

INDIAN OCEAN

AUSTRALIA

AUSTRALIAN PLATE

Fiji Is.

Tonga Is.

South I.

North I.

IF YOU WANT TO SEE SOME
REAL TECTONIC-PLATE ACTION, HEAD TO A
DESTINATION IN THE RING OF FIRE, WHICH

stretches around the rim of the Pacific Ocean. It's where more than 75 percent of Earth's volcanoes erupt and 80 percent of all earthquakes occur. The reason? Several of Earth's tectonic plates come together around the ring. The plates crash into each other, and the edges shift over or under each other. The collisions release a huge amount of energy.

ABBREVIATIONS

I .... Island
Is. .... Islands
St. .... Saint
U.S.A. .... United States of America

ANTARCTIC

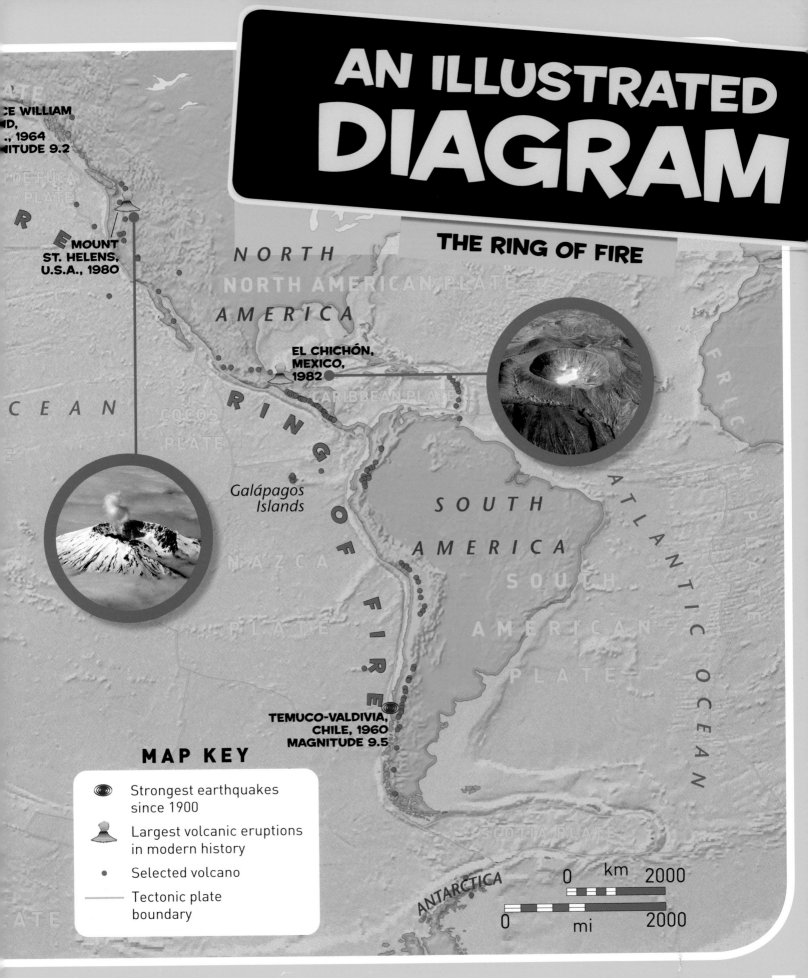

AN ILLUSTRATED DIAGRAM

THE RING OF FIRE

CE WILLIAM
ND,
., 1964
ITUDE 9.2

MOUNT
ST. HELENS,
U.S.A., 1980

DE FUCA
PLATE

R
E

CEAN

NORTH

NORTH AMERICAN PLATE

AMERICA

COCOS
PLATE

EL CHICHÓN,
MEXICO,
1982

CARIBBEAN PLATE

R
I
N
G

O
F

F
I
R
E

Galápagos
Islands

NAZCA

PLATE

SOUTH

AMERICA

SOUTH

AMERICAN

PLATE

ATLANTIC OCEAN

RICA
PLATE

TEMUCO-VALDIVIA,
CHILE, 1960
MAGNITUDE 9.5

MAP KEY

- Strongest earthquakes since 1900
- Largest volcanic eruptions in modern history
- Selected volcano
- Tectonic plate boundary

ANTARCTICA

SCOTIA PLATE

0   km   2000

0   mi   2000

ATE

Volcanologists study the lava spewing from Mount Etna, in Sicily, Italy. The volcano is in an almost constant state of activity and is one of the most active volcanoes in the world.

2
VOLCANO POWER

A HOT TOPIC

WHAT GOES ON INSIDE

A STEAMING, BREWING VOLCANO? If you could look inside a volcano, you'd see something that looks like a long pipe, called a conduit. It leads from inside the magma chamber under the crust up to a vent, or opening, at the top of the mountain. Some conduits have branches that shoot off to the side, called fissures.

When pressure builds from gases inside the volcano, the gases must find an escape, and they head up toward the surface! An eruption occurs when lava, gases, ash, and rocks explode out of the vent.

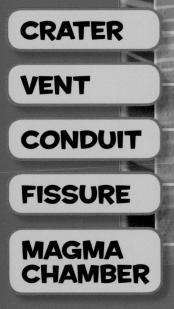

CRATER

VENT

CONDUIT

FISSURE

MAGMA CHAMBER

HARDENED LAVA AND ASH LAYERS

TYPES OF VOLCANOES

CINDER CONE VOLCANO
Eve's Cone, Canada

Cinder cone volcanoes look like an upside-down ice-cream cone. They spew out cinder and hot ash. Some of these volcanoes smoke and erupt for years at a time.

COMPOSITE VOLCANO
Licancábur, Chile

Composite volcanoes, or stratovolcanoes, form as lava, ash, and cinder from previous eruptions harden and build up over time. These volcanoes spit out pyroclastic flows, or thick explosions of hot ash that travel at hundreds of miles (km) an hour.

SHIELD VOLCANO
Mauna Loa, Hawaii, U.S.A.

The gentle, broad slopes of a shield volcano look like an ancient warrior's shield. Its eruptions are often slower. Lava splatters and bubbles rather than shooting forcefully into the air.

LAVA DOME VOLCANO
Mount St. Helens, Washington, U.S.A.

Dome volcanoes have steep sides. Hardened lava often plugs the vent at the top of a dome volcano. Pressure builds beneath the surface until the top blows.

HOT SPOTS
Some volcanoes form at hot spots, or holes beneath Earth's crust in the middle of a tectonic plate. As lava pushes up through the hole and forms a volcanic island, the plate keeps moving. More volcanoes form as it moves. Some hot spots are big enough to create a chain of volcanic islands, such as the Hawaiian Islands.

COLLAPSE!
An erupting volcano can cause damage to itself! A caldera is a large bowl-like depression caused by the collapse of a magma chamber during an eruption. Crater Lake in Oregon, U.S.A., is a caldera that has filled with rainwater and snowfall.

EXPLOSIVE FACT
A GALLON OF VOLCANIC ASH IS TEN TIMES HEAVIER THAN A GALLON OF SNOW!

UNDERWATER ACTION

A deep-water submersible explores the El Bajo Seamount, an underwater point off the coast of Central America.

THE HEAT PRODUCED
AT EARTH'S CORE GIVES RISE

to some mysterious goings-on down deep, where only submarines and ROVs (remotely operated vehicles that are directed underwater by an operator aboard a boat) go. With the help of some high-tech devices, scientists are going to depths of 16,000 feet (5,000 m) to film, scrape, and sample the ocean floor. With their help, we're learning a lot about underwater volcanoes.

EXTREME LIFE-FORMS

Tube worms thrive in the heat and consume the bacteria around hydrothermal vents. Specially adapted to the dark, scalding-hot, and toxic environment, tube worms can grow to be eight feet (2.4 m) long.

HYDROTHERMAL VENTS

Hot springs on the ocean floor gush mineral-rich fluids through hydrothermal vents. These vents are formed when plates under the ocean move apart. Seawater seeps into the cracks and is heated by the molten rock beneath.

A black smoker is a blast of water as hot as 750°F (400°C) that shoots out of a hydrothermal vent. The water looks like black smoke because it is full of sulfur.

STINKY GAS

Sulfur from El Hierro, an underwater volcano in the Canary Islands, turned the surrounding waters bright green.

SPREADING SEAFLOOR

Scientists are always tracking plate movements at the bottom of the ocean floor. Underwater volcanic mountain ranges, called mid-ocean ridges, rise up where the edges of plates push together. Meanwhile, slowly but steadily, the continents are spreading apart. The spreading seafloor may be widening Earth's oceans by about an inch (2.5 cm) each year.

EXPLOSIVE FACT MARS HAS A VOLCANO NAMED OLYMPUS MONS THAT IS AS WIDE AS THE U.S. STATE OF ARIZONA.

SMOKIN' FACTS ABOUT VOLCANOES

WHAT DO YOU CALL SOMEONE WHO CAN'T GET ENOUGH OF VOLCANOES?

A volcanologist. That's a scientist who studies volcanoes and watches their activity —sometimes at very close range. Volcanologists learn a lot from studying volcanoes before—as well as after—eruptions. For example, they monitor active and dormant volcanoes for temperature changes and emission of sulfur and other toxic gases. The data they gather provide clues about when a volcano may be ready to blow its top. Their work saves lives. Here are some cool facts about volcanoes that will make you feel like a volcanologist.

A volcanologist wears a protective suit to study volcanoes.

Eyjafjallajökull volcano, Iceland

VOLCANO LIGHTNING

You can see lightning in the middle of a volcanic ash cloud—it sparks when particles collide, creating friction and an electrical charge.

LAVA CAVES

Sometimes a lava flow stops, cools, and hollows out, leaving a tunnel where people can hike.

ACID LAKES

Lakes in volcano craters can contain water so concentrated with gases that it can burn through flesh in minutes!

[top photo] Mount St. Helens National Volcanic Monument, Washington, U.S.A.
[middle photo] Lake Nyos, Cameroon
[bottom photo] Mount Tambora, Indonesia

A YEAR WITHOUT SUMMER

The 1815 volcanic blast on Mount Tambora, in Indonesia, is the largest volcanic eruption in recorded history. Ash and dust spread around the globe, blocking the summer sun and causing a "volcanic winter."

EXPLORER'S CORNER

Volcanologists suit up in some pretty high-tech gear when they get up close and personal with the inside of an active volcano—and when I go with them to get shots of their work, so do I. Our suits, coated with aluminum, were first developed by NASA in the 1950s to protect astronauts, but come in handy—like full-body oven mitts—near lakes of molten rock, too! The aluminum helps bounce heat rays off, and layers underneath insulate us in temperatures as high as 500°F (260°C). We need air tanks and breathing apparatus, helmets with special glass lenses, and, of course, special gloves and boots. Even my cameras are custom-made!

THE UPSIDE OF VOLCANOES

VOLCANOES AREN'T ALL BAD NEWS.

They provide many rich resources. Soil made from volcanic material promotes healthy plant life. Geothermal power, which comes from heat inside the Earth, is a renewable energy source that can power homes and factories. In fact, about 70 percent of Iceland's energy comes from volcanic geothermal power. Volcanoes offer luxurious resources, too. Valuable minerals and precious gems are the work of volcanoes. Mud baths and mineral spas are some of the unique by-products of the natural power of volcanoes.

AHHHHH! In Iceland's Blue Lagoon, at the base of a geothermal power plant, tourists soak in nature's hot tub, heated by lava fields.

EXPLOSIVE FACT IN JAPAN, SNOW MONKEYS WARM UP IN WINTER BY SOAKING IN VOLCANIC HOT SPRINGS.

MUD MASK

Your skin won't get clean in this bath, but it'll sure look good afterward! Mineral-rich volcanic mud draws tourists to lots of spas in New Zealand.

BURIED TREASURE

When solid magma spews out of volcanic vents, it sometimes carries kimberlite with it, a rare blue rock that occasionally contains diamonds.

RUB-A-DUB-DUB

Pumice, a volcanic rock, is the lightest rock on Earth. It even floats in water. Many people rub their skin with pumice when they bathe to soften or remove hard skin on elbows and feet.

A PHOTO GALLERY

THE POWER OF

MOTHER NATURE IS SCARY AND AMAZING. Whether we see them in action or witness the aftermath, earthquakes and volcanoes change the shape of our planet and capture our imagination.

Arenal Volcano, in Alajuela, Costa Rica, erupts at dusk.

An aerial view captures an image of the Danakil Depression, a crater in Ethiopia and part of the Great Rift Valley.

Giant's Causeway in Northern Ireland contains basalt columns created by an ancient eruption.

A fracture in the Earth lies next to volcanic cones in Great Rift Valley, Djibouti, in Africa.

Lava flows from Fimmvorouhals volcano in Iceland.

snapshot of Russia's Kamchatka Peninsula, taken from space, shows four volcanoes erupting at once.

Lava fountains bubble inside the crater of Mount Etna in Sicily, Italy.

Three years after a devastating earthquake in Port-au-Prince, Haiti, much damage remains.

Mount Hood in Oregon, U.S.A., is reflected in the waters of Trillium Lake.

Tofua Island, Tonga, has a freshwater lake inside the volcano's caldera.

Human engineering can be no match for a powerful earthquake. When a strong quake strikes, structures can buckle and crumble in an instant. In 1995, an earthquake destroyed this highway in Osaka, Kobe, Japan.

3

SHAKE, RATTLE, & ROLL

KNOW YOUR QUAKES

In 2012, a 6.9 magnitude earthquake destroyed homes and villages in the central Philippines.

THE AMOUNT OF ENERGY GENERATED BY AN EARTHQUAKE IN THE INDIAN OCEAN IN 2004 COULD HAVE POWERED ALL U.S. HOMES AND BUSINESSES FOR THREE DAYS.

THE SPOT WHERE AN EARTHQUAKE RUPTURES IS CALLED ITS EPICENTER.

Vibrations called seismic waves travel out around the epicenter in circles, like ripples from a rock tossed into a lake. People living hundreds of miles from the epicenter can sometimes feel the Earth shudder beneath their feet.

People have tried to predict earthquakes for thousands of years. Knowing when an earthquake will happen can help people prepare for disaster. Scientists are still developing tools to measure the power, duration, and direction of an earthquake because these are clues to what might happen in the future.

MOMENT MAGNITUDE SCALE

The moment magnitude scale measures the size of an earthquake by the amount of energy it releases. Developed in the 1970s by Thomas Hanks and Hiroo Kanamori, the scale is a successor to the Richter scale. Here's how to rate a quake:

10+ has not been recorded

9 severe—occurs once every 5 to 20 years

8 serious damage over a large area

7 serious damage to buildings and structures

6 strong enough to be destructive

5 moderate damage over a small area

4 minor damage—occurs daily around the world

3 often felt but rarely causes damage

2 (or less) not usually felt, but recorded by seismographs

TRACKING EARTHQUAKES

A seismograph can measure and record the strength of the seismic waves that move away from the quake's epicenter. It detects the smallest changes in Earth's movements. The device converts the movements into electronic signals that are recorded by a computer. Scientists combine the data from several seismographs to locate the quake's epicenter and figure out how deep and strong the quake is.

ANCIENT EARTHQUAKE DETECTOR

Zhang Hen was a Chinese inventor who lived from A.D. 78–139. Historians credit him with constructing the world's first seismometer, shown here. When the ground shook, a ball fell from the dragon's head into a toad-shaped container below. The device showed the direction of the quake's epicenter.

By the Numbers

500,000 quakes are detected around the globe each year.

100,000 quakes are strong enough to be felt by people each year.

100 quakes are strong enough to cause some damage each year.

3 quakes are strong enough to cause serious damage over large areas each year.

CAN ANIMALS PREDICT EARTHQUAKES?

ARE ANIMALS
TRYING TO TELL US SOMETHING WHEN THEY SEEM TO GO WILD FOR NO REASON?

It turns out that animals may be more sensitive to vibrations and chemical changes in rocks and air than humans are. As far back as 373 B.C., people reported seeing rats, snakes, and weasels fleeing a city in Greece just days before a devastating earthquake.

In 1975, hibernating snakes slithered out of their winter burrows and high-tailed it out of Haicheng, China. One month later a large earthquake shook the city. Even elephants are tuned in to quakes. Just hours before a tremendous tsunami hit Thailand in 2004, anxious elephants ran to higher ground. Since scientists can't create earthquakes in a lab, it's difficult to prove that animals are accurate predictors of natural disasters. Even so, it probably makes sense to pay attention to animals when they start acting strange.

EXPLOSIVE FACT IN 1989 A GEOLOGIST PREDICTED THE SAN FRANCISCO EARTHQUAKE A WEEK BEFORE IT OCCURRED WHEN HE NOTICED A LARGE NUMBER OF MISSING PET NOTICES IN THE LOCAL CLASSIFIED ADS.

SNAKE ALERT

Three days before Mount Pelée erupted on the island of Martinique in 1902, dozens of pit vipers appeared in the town of St. Pierre, killing some 50 people and 200 animals with their venomous bites. Centipedes and ants also left their mountain homes before Pelée blew.

NO EGGS TODAY

Farmers are tuned in to their chickens, and the birds may be tuned in to earthquake warning signs. Over the years, many farmers have reported that chickens stop laying eggs before large earthquakes.

Asian elephants

EXPLORER'S CORNER

Scientists see evidence of fault movement in some unlikely places. California's San Andreas Fault (background image) runs through forests of redwoods (inset), the planet's tallest trees. Some trunks show distinct zigzags as they reach toward the sky. And deep in one forest stands a stump split down the middle by an earthquake. It's the size of a small living room, and the gap in the middle, right in line with the fault, is big enough for a man to climb in.

EXPLOSIVE FACT
THE MOVEMENTS OF PLATES ALONG CALIFORNIA'S SAN ANDREAS FAULT ARE SLOWLY MOVING LOS ANGELES AND SAN FRANCISCO CLOSER TOGETHER. THEY COULD BE NEIGHBORS IN SEVERAL MILLION YEARS.

LIVING ON THE FAULT LINE

EARTHQUAKES CAN MAKE LIFE DIFFICULT

for months and even years after they occur. A massive quake can destroy roads, bridges, and airport runways. When this happens, people can't get the food or supplies they need. However, with the right training and advance planning, people can survive big jolts safely.

TSUNAMI EVACUATION ROUTE

HERE WE GO AGAIN

The 2011 earthquake in Japan hit 9.0 on the magnitude scale and then produced more than 400 aftershock quakes with a magnitude of at least 5 or greater!

TSUNAMI WARNINGS

When earthquakes occur at the bottom of the ocean, the aftershocks reach far and wide from the epicenter. Many coastal cities have tsunami warning systems that set off alarms that warn residents to flee coastal areas. The alarms are triggered by signals from special buoys out at sea that sense changes in sea level after an underwater earthquake.

LOOK TO THE WATER

Aftershocks can make waves in a pond or swimming pool roll back and forth. The phenomenon is called a seiche (pronounced saysh) or standing wave.

ALWAYS LEARNING

Scientists at the Oregon State University Wave Research Laboratory in Oregon, U.S.A., have built the ultimate wave machine. The tsunami wave basin simulates the powerful waves made by a tsunami, so we can better understand beach erosion and coastal flooding.

BRACE YOURSELF

SAN FRANCISCO'S TRANSAMERICA PYRAMID HAS A 52-FOOT-DEEP (16 M) FOUNDATION THAT CAN SHIFT WITH THE MOTION OF AN EARTHQUAKE.

MILLIONS OF PEOPLE LIVE
IN AREAS THAT ARE PRONE TO EARTHQUAKES.

For them, learning how to stay safe during a quake is a necessity. They need to be in specially designed buildings and protected from falling objects and shattering glass.

A HELPING HAND

It takes many volunteers to help people after a natural disaster. Rescuing survivors from the rubble is difficult and dangerous. Organizations such as the Red Cross and other "first responders" help save countless lives. When homes are destroyed, organizations and volunteers also help people find shelters with the necessary food, water, and supplies.

LIKE THE REAL THING

Earthquake simulators are close to the real thing. They produce effects in a van or room that are similar to quakes with magnitudes of 3 to 8. People can learn safety measures by using simulators to practice avoiding injuries. Architects and engineers also learn good design principles with these tools.

STRONGER BUILDINGS

This 55-story building in Mexico City, Mexico, withstood a 7.6 magnitude quake in January 2003. Architects believe it can withstand up to an 8.5 magnitude quake. The first 30 floors are made of 21,000 tons (19,051 t) of steel reinforced in concrete. The upper floors have steel columns that are able to sway. Architects believe that when the upper floors can sway a bit, buildings are safer from shaking and rattling below.

EXPLOSIVE FACT IN 2010 A MASSIVE 8.8 QUAKE MOVED A CITY IN CHILE TEN FEET (3 M) TO THE WEST AND SLIGHTLY TIPPED EARTH ON ITS AXIS.

EARTHSHAKING
COMPARISONS

EARTHQUAKES AND VOLCANOES CAN UNLEASH UNBELIEVABLE

amounts of force and energy. Take a look at how Earth's awesome action measures up to things you're familiar with.

KRAKATAU, 1883

This volcanic eruption in Indonesia released energy equal to 13,000 times the nuclear yield of the bomb that hit Hiroshima in World War II.

HOW HOT IS LAVA?

The average temperature of lava is about 2000°F (1100°C). That's four times hotter than the hottest setting of a kitchen oven!

EXPLOSIVE FACT PEOPLE HEARD THE BLAST FROM THE 1883 ERUPTION OF KRAKATAU SOME 2,900 MILES (4,653 KM) AWAY.

HOW FAST DOES A TSUNAMI TRAVEL?

In deep ocean waters, a tsunami moves as fast as a jet plane.

HOW FAST DOES A TECTONIC PLATE MOVE?

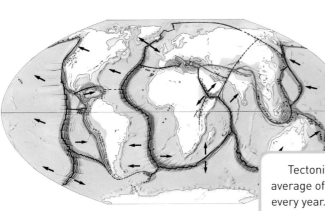

Tectonic plates move at an average of about an inch (2.5 cm) every year. Your hair grows about six times faster than that!

HOW MUCH ENERGY DOES AN EARTHQUAKE RELEASE?

An earthquake with a magnitude of 9 releases as much energy as 99 million tons of dynamite.

Volcanoes, like this one in Indonesia, have become popular tourist destinations for people looking for "adventure travel."

4
HAVE A BLAST!

THE STUFF OF LEGENDS

LONG BEFORE

PEOPLE UNDERSTOOD WHAT CAUSED NATURE'S FURY, THEY created legends about fiery volcanoes and Earth's angry tremors. These colorful stories tried to make sense of an unpredictable world. From one generation to the next, the stories were told and retold. Even today, artists, writers, and storytellers are inspired by the powers of nature. It's a long tradition.

VULCAN

More than 2,000 years ago, the Romans worshipped Vulcan, the Roman god of fire. They believed that Vulcan controlled destructive fires, especially volcanoes. People prayed to this deity when they wanted to stay safe from fire. To keep the god happy, they built temples to honor him. Vulcan was good at making things, using fire to forge metal objects. He married Venus, the goddess of love and beauty.

PELE, HAWAIIAN GODDESS OF FIRE

Don't anger the Hawaiian goddess Pele! People say she lives in the crater of Kilauea, on the island of Hawaii. She controls the lava and has the ability to destroy anything in her path. Still, some people say she is kind and call her "She Who Shapes the Sacred Land." According to legend, Pele can take the form of a beautiful young woman, or an old woman with a white dog.

LAVA LAMP

To make a groovy lava lamp, first you'll need a tall jar.

1 Pour about 6 inches (15 cm) of water into the jar.

2 Add 2/3 cup of vegetable oil.

3 Wait until the oil rises to the top. Then add two drops of red food coloring to the oil.

4 To make your oily "lava" flow, shake some salt into the jar. Continue adding salt for as long as you want to make the bubbles sink and float in the water. Place the jar in front of a lamp for best results.

WHAT JUST HAPPENED?

Your lava lamp doesn't contain real lava—it just looks like it. Here's how it works. The oil floats on the water because it is less dense. The salt is denser, so it sinks to the bottom, pulling some oil along with it. As the salt dissolves, the oil floats back to the top. Now you have a cool lava flow that won't burn your hands!

Great Heights

30,080 FEET (9,170 m) is the height of Mauna Loa volcano, which makes up part of Hawaii. It begins below the ocean.

19,341 FEET (5,895 m) is the height of Kilimanjaro, the tallest mountain in Africa—and also a volcano.

19 MILES (30 km) is the height reached by the ash cloud over the volcano Hekla, in Iceland, in a 1947 eruption.

1,640 FEET (500 m) is the height to which some lava fountains rose in the eruption of Askja, a volcano in Iceland.

THE AMAZING VANISHING CITY

YOU MAY HAVE HEARD THE STORY OF THE LOST CITY OF ATLANTIS. IT IS ONE OF THOSE AMAZING

mysteries that historians and scientists continue to debate. Around 360 B.C., Greek philosopher Plato wrote about an island that was lost forever under the Atlantic Ocean. It took just one day and one night, he wrote, for the ancient city to be lost to the sea. It was not until the 1800s when someone studied global flood histories and realized that Plato's story may be partly true.

Statue of Plato

COULD PLATO'S STORY BE TRUE?

Plato described Atlantis as a city built on a hill surrounded by water, with tunnels and canals for ships. Huge fields and farms fed a great civilization. Plato lived from 427 B.C. to 347 B.C. It turns out that one of the biggest volcanic eruptions since the last ice age happened on the Greek island of Santorini, in about 1620 B.C. That huge eruption probably caused the demise of an entire civilization, called the Minoans, and caused the volcano's caldera to sink underwater. This eruption may have sparked the legendary story.

OTHER WILD THEORIES

Not everyone agrees with the theory that Atlantis may have been part of the Greek islands. Other theories suggest that the city was located in Bolivia, near the Andes Mountains. Still others say that the city was near an island off the coast of Florida. The rest of the debaters claim that Central America, the China Sea, or Africa are the real locations of this legendary city.

An artist's concept of the Lost City of Atlantis

THE WORLD IN YOUR HANDS

Learning about earthquakes and volcanoes can include some hands-on fun. Geologists like to head into the field to get dirty. You, too, can shake some things up, as long as you don't do anything too explosive or dangerous! Here are some activities you can do at home to help experience some of the effects of Earth's rattling, rocking powers.

MAKING MOUNTAINS

1 Place a piece of construction paper on a table and, down the center of the paper, draw a mountain range. Name the range, and make some mountains larger than others.

2 Place one hand on either side of the paper. Slowly push your hands toward each other to see how the mountain range rises and changes.

WHAT JUST HAPPENED?

What you're doing with your hands is the same as pushing tectonic plates together, causing the edges to crumple up against each other. Many earthquakes and volcanoes are found along mountain ranges like the one you've drawn. If you were to do this demonstration in real time, you would have to move your hands about an inch (2.5 cm) a year. That's how slowly Earth's plates really move.

Modern-day Santorini

EXPLOSIVE FACT IN GREEK MYTHOLOGY, POSEIDON, GOD OF SEA AND EARTHQUAKES, HAD A SON WHO WAS BORN IN THE CITY OF ATLANTIS.

EARTH SMARTS

GEOLOGISTS USE MOMENT MAGNITUDE TO MEASURE THE MAGNITUDE
of earthquakes, and they use something called the Volcanic Explosivity Index (VEI) to rate volcanoes. The VEI relies on a combination of variables—such as the volume of all lava, ash, and rock produced by the eruption. A zero on the scale means the eruption was nonexplosive, and an eight means an ash cloud over 31 miles (50 km) high!

YOU RATE IT

Match the earthquake damage to the moment magnitude scale number.

A 1–3 MAGNITUDE

B 4–5 MAGNITUDE

C 6–8 MAGNITUDE

VOLCANO MATCH-UP

TEST YOUR KNOWLEDGE

about the different kinds of volcanoes you've read about in this book. Hopefully this game won't make you blow your top! Match each photo to the correct type of volcano.

1

2

A CINDER CONE VOLCANO

....

B SHIELD VOLCANO

....

C COMPOSITE VOLCANO

....

D LAVA DOME

4

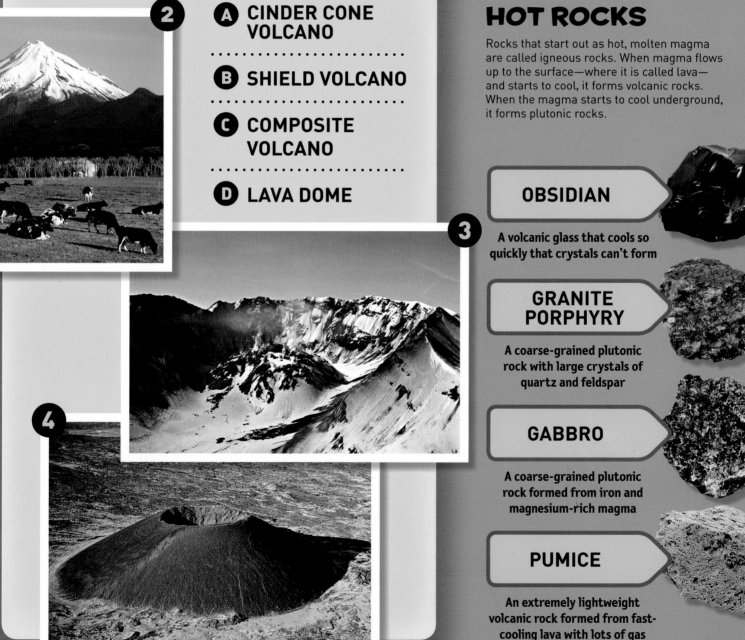

HOT ROCKS

Rocks that start out as hot, molten magma are called igneous rocks. When magma flows up to the surface—where it is called lava—and starts to cool, it forms volcanic rocks. When the magma starts to cool underground, it forms plutonic rocks.

3

OBSIDIAN

A volcanic glass that cools so quickly that crystals can't form

GRANITE PORPHYRY

A coarse-grained plutonic rock with large crystals of quartz and feldspar

GABBRO

A coarse-grained plutonic rock formed from iron and magnesium-rich magma

PUMICE

An extremely lightweight volcanic rock formed from fast-cooling lava with lots of gas

EXPLOSIVE FACT
THE LARGEST MUDFLOW EVER—98 FEET (30 M) THICK—BEGAN ATOP MOUNT RAINIER IN WASHINGTON STATE, U.S.A.

POP CULTURE
DISASTERS

1

A

MATCH THE
PLACE ON THE LEFT
with the movie on the right
that's associated with it.

2

B

1 Ngauruhoe

This is the youngest of a volcanic
trio that rises in the heart of New
Zealand's Tongariro National Park.
It seems almost magical in the
perfect symmetry of its cone.

2 Washington, D.C.

In 2011, an earthquake made
the Washington Monument in
Washington, D.C., U.S.A., shake
and rattle, leaving a crack in the
monument. It was just a coinci-
dence that two years earlier a movie
had come out in which a natural
disaster struck Washington, D.C.

3

C

3 Mount Etna

This is an active volcano on the east
coast of Sicily. It is the tallest active
volcano in Europe and one of the
most active volcanoes in the world.

CRUST

MANTLE

OUTER CORE

INNER CORE

A — Star Wars Episode III: Revenge of the Sith

A volcano starred as a part of the landscape on the planet Mustafar in the 2005 film *Star Wars Episode III: Revenge of the Sith*.
Hint: The camera crew might have enjoyed pasta on location.

B — The Lord of the Rings

In J.R.R. Tolkien's *The Lord of the Rings* trilogy, Mount Doom is the volcano where the magical "ring to rule them all," with its dark powers, was created—and it's the only place where the ring can be destroyed.
Hint: The trilogy was filmed in a country below the Equator.

C — 2012

In the movie *2012*, a man fights to save his family from massive earthquakes that throw cities into the ocean, knock down famous landmarks, and threaten to destroy the planet.

WHAT'S DOWN BELOW?

Match each layer of Earth to its description.

A. This is the perfect place to gaze at 1,800 miles (2,897 km) of dense liquid rock.

. . . .

B. It's many miles of solid rock, but can still be compared to the skin of an apple.

. . . .

C. Iron and nickel make up this deep layer of Earth.

. . . .

D. Liquid iron and nickel is most of the scenery in this hot zone.

ANSWERS: A: mantle, B: crust, C: inner core, D: outer core

EXPLOSIVE FACT TONGARIRO, A NEIGHBOR OF NGAURUHOE, REALLY ERUPTED IN NOVEMBER 2012.

PHOTO FINISH

DON'T GO JUMP IN *THIS* LAKE!

IT'S A QUARTER MILE (0.4 KM) DOWN FROM THE

rim of Nyiragongo, a volcano in the center of Africa. What was I doing there? I was working with scientists who are desperate to learn as much as they can as fast as they can about this volcano. Why? Because it's only a matter of time before it erupts, and close to a million people live right by its base. By looking inside to study Nyiragongo's rocks, sample its gases, and watch how it works, scientists hope to answer a big question: When?

After a day of hiking, we reached Nyiragongo's rim, over 11,000 feet (3.4 km) high. Even up there we could feel the heat of the lava in the lake below, exploding in fiery orange geysers. It was an amazing sight. Pretty terrifying too.

But we had scarier stuff to do. Wearing gas masks and other special equipment (check my Explorer's Corner on page 27), we made our way with ropes down the inner walls of the crater and set up camp on a wide ledge 800 feet (244 m) down. The air (if you could call it that) was filled with acid and metal particles.

There on the ledge, the scientists set up a field laboratory to measure all the toxic gases. By monitoring the gases and measuring changes in their chemical makeup, they might be able, over time, to find clues about what leads to an eruption. That means they'll need to make regular return visits. Chances are I won't be with them. I made it all the way down to the crater floor, to within feet of the edge of the roiling, bubbling, lava lake. Been there, done that!

Carsten Peter poses in a safe spot during his field-work at Nyiragongo.

AFTERWORD

ANIMALS TO THE RESCUE

HUMANS AREN'T THE ONLY
VOLUNTEERS RUSHING TO THE RESCUE AFTER
natural disasters like earthquakes and volcanoes.

Search and rescue dogs train for many specialized tasks, but one of the most important is to sniff both the air and the ground for signs of life. What exactly are they trained to identify? They can smell the microscopic skin cells that humans shed constantly. Dogs travel with firefighters, police, and other special handlers—and save many lives after disasters.

Smaller animals come in handy, too. Would you believe cockroaches with cameras? You bet. Six-legged creepy crawlers carry audio and video equipment into places that are too small or too dangerous for rescue dogs. Scientists use low-grade electrical pulses to steer the roaches around obstacles and into places where people may be trapped. Rescue crews can then analyze feedback and decide which areas to dig out first, and which areas need to be cleared with extra care.

A cockroach loaded with audio and video equipment is a little bigger than a quarter.

This rescue worker and trained pup are searching for survivors of a massive earthquake and tsunami that hit Japan in March 2011.

Worried that volcanic ash from Iceland's Eyjafjallajökull volcano would damage airplanes, air travel was shut down for about a week in 2010 in many European countries.

AN INTERACTIVE GLOSSARY

A helicopter hovers over the erupting Kilauea volcano in Hawaii.

PEOPLE WHO STUDY VOLCANOES AND EARTHQUAKES USE THESE WORDS.

Check the glossary to see what each word means, and visit its page numbers to see how the word is used in context. Then test whether your knowledge is a bit shaky or rock solid.

Caldera
(PAGES 22–23)
A large depression in a volcano caused by the collapse of a magma chamber during an eruption

What forms when a caldera fills with rainwater?
a. quicksand
b. a lake
c. mountains
d. lava

Composite volcano
(PAGES 22–23)
A volcanic mountain formed by hardened layers of lava, ash, and cinder from previous eruptions

What happens to a composite volcano over time?
a. It gets taller.
b. It gets hotter.
c. It is struck by lightning.
d. It erupts more often.

Dormant volcano
(PAGE 26)
A volcano that has not erupted since the last ice age, but is expected to erupt again

Which word best describes something that is dormant?
a. melted
b. noisy
c. active
d. asleep

Fissure
(PAGES 22–23)
A smaller pipe that shoots off from the side of a volcano's central pipe

Which analogy best describes a fissure? A fissure is to a volcano as
a. perfume is to air
b. an ice cube is to water
c. a branch is to a tree
d. a bird is to a bush

Geothermal energy
(PAGES 28–29)
Energy that is made from the heat in Earth's interior

Which of these is a source of geothermal energy?
a. earthquakes
b. volcanoes
c. tsunamis
d. landslides

Hydrothermal vent
(PAGES 24–25)
An opening in the seafloor through which hot, mineral-rich water flows

Under what kind of conditions will you find a hydrothermal vent?
a. dark and hot
b. bright and cold
c. dry and windy
d. fertile and shady

Lava
(PAGES 10–11)
What magma is called when it reaches the outside of a volcano

When are you likely to find lava in its hot, molten state?
a. during a tsunami
b. during an earthquake
c. during a volcanic eruption
d. during an aftershock

Magma
(PAGES 10–11)
Molten rock inside a volcano's vent, before it reaches the surface

Where on Earth would you NOT likely find magma?
a. at a hot spot
b. along the Ring of Fire
c. in a volcano vent
d. on top of a fault line

Molten
(PAGES 10–11)
Liquefied by heat, such as rock that is found beneath Earth's surface

In which layer of Earth would you find molten rock?
a. crust
b. mantle
c. inner core
d. outer core

Moment magnitude scale
(PAGES 34–35)
Developed by Thomas Hanks and Hiroo Kanamori, the moment magnitude scale measures the size of an earthquake by the amount of energy it releases.

Which is the best description for a 9.5 earthquake on the magnitude scale?
a. mild
b. average
c. strong
d. disastrous

Seismograph
(PAGES 34–35)
An instrument that detects small movements in Earth's crust

Where do seismograph signals come from?
a. hurricanes
b. tsunamis
c. earthquakes
d. volcanoes

Tectonic plate
(PAGES 10–11, 18–19)
One of the many plates that make up Earth's crust, each one able to shift and move

Where is the most tectonic plate movement on Earth?
a. Mid-Atlantic Ridge
b. Ring of Fire
c. Hawaiian Islands
d. Mount St. Helens

Tsunami
(PAGES 16–17)
A large wave caused by earthquakes or large volcanic eruptions under the ocean

Why are tsunamis dangerous to humans?
a. They move fast.
b. They carry tons of debris.
c. They flood coastal cities.
d. All of the above.

ANSWERS: caldera: **b.** composite volcano: **a.** dormant volcano: **d.** fissure: **c.** geothermal energy: **b.** hydrothermal vent: **a.** lava: **c.** magma: **d.** molten: **b.** moment magnitude scale: **d.** seismograph: **c.** tectonic plate: **b.** tsunami: **d**

FIND OUT MORE

BOOKS

Jump Into Science: Earthquakes
BY ELLEN J. PRAGER
National Geographic, 2007

National Geographic Readers: Volcanoes
BY ANNE SCHREIBER
National Geographic, 2008

National Geographic Science Chapters: Rivers of Fire: The Story of Volcanoes
BY MONICA HELPERN
National Geographic, 2006

Witness to Disaster: Earthquakes
BY JUDY FRADIN AND DENNIS FRADIN
National Geographic, 2008

Witness to Disaster: Volcanoes
BY JUDY FRADIN AND DENNIS FRADIN
National Geographic, 2007

MOVIES TO WATCH

Doomsday Volcano
National Geographic, 2007

L.A.'s Future Quake
National Geographic, 2006

Man vs. Volcano
National Geographic, 2011

National Geographic Classics: Forces of Nature
National Geographic, 2010

Violent Earth
National Geographic, 2006

WEBSITES

U.S. Geological Survey: Earthquakes for Kids
earthquake.usgs.gov/learn/kids/

U.S. Geological Survey: Volcano Hazards Program
volcanoes.usgs.gov/

Weather Wiz Kids: Volcanoes
www.weatherwizkids.com/weather-volcano.htm

Weather Wiz Kids: Earthquakes
www.weatherwizkids.com/weather-earthquake.htm

Volcano World for Kids
volcano.oregonstate.edu/oldroot/kids/

Volcanoes: Earth's fiery power
environment.nationalgeographic.com/environment/natural-disasters/volcano-profile/

PLACES TO VISIT

Arenal National Park, Costa Rica
Bromo-Tengger-Semeru National Park, East Java, Indonesia
Kilauea Volcano, Hawaii, U.S.A.
Mount Fuji, Japan
Mount Pacaya, Guatemala
Mount St. Helens, Washington State, U.S.A.
Vesuvius National Park, Italy
Yellowstone National Park, Idaho, Montana, and Wyoming, U.S.A.

Published by the National Geographic Society
John M. Fahey, Jr., *Chairman of the Board
and Chief Executive Officer*
Declan Moore, *Executive Vice President; President, Publishing
and Travel*
Melina Gerosa Bellows, *Executive Vice President;
Chief Creative Officer, Books, Kids, and Family*

Prepared by the Book Division
Hector Sierra, *Senior Vice President and General Manager*
Nancy Laties Feresten, *Senior Vice President,
Kids Publishing and Media*
Jay Sumner, *Director of Photography, Children's Publishing*
Jennifer Emmett, *Vice President, Editorial Director, Children's
Books*
Eva Absher-Schantz, *Design Director, Kids Publishing and Media*
R. Gary Colbert, *Production Director*
Jennifer A. Thornton, *Director of Managing Editorial*

Staff for This Book
Lynn Addison, Robin Terry, *Project Editors*
James Hiscott, Jr., *Art Director*
Annette Kiesow, *Illustrations Editor*
Joanna Wojtkowiak, *Designer*
Marisa Larson, *Researcher*
Callie Broaddus, *Design Production Assistant*
Hillary Moloney, *Associate Photo Editor*
Carl Mehler, *Director of Maps*
Matt Chwastyk, *Map Research and Production*
Grace Hill, *Associate Managing Editor*
Joan Gossett, *Production Editor*
Lewis R. Bassford, *Production Manager*
Susan Borke, *Legal and Business Affairs*

Production Services
Phillip L. Schlosser, *Senior Vice President*
Chris Brown, *Vice President, NG Book Manufacturing*
George Bounelis, *Vice President, Production Services*
Nicole Elliott, *Manager*
Rachel Faulise, *Manager*
Robert L. Barr, *Manager*

Captions
Cover: Kilauea on the Big Island of Hawaii is one of the world's most
active volcanoes. The word Kilauea means "spewing" in the Hawaiian
language.
Page 1: This giant crack in a roadway in Tarlay, Shan State, in
northeastern Myanmar, was caused by a 6.8 magnitude earthquake,
which knocked down 130 houses in the same area.
Pages 2–3: A tsunami, which followed a 9.0 magnitude earthquake,
caused water to flow into the city of Miyako, Iwate, Japan, in March
2011.
Back cover: Mount Pinatubo, Luzon, in the Philippines, erupted in
1991, producing avalanches, mudflows, and a giant volcanic ash cloud.

The National Geographic Society is one of the
world's largest nonprofit scientific and educational
organizations. Founded in 1888 to "increase and
diffuse geographic knowledge," the Society works
to inspire people to care about the planet. National
Geographic reflects the world through its magazines,
television programs, films, music and radio, books,
DVDs, maps, exhibitions, live events, school publishing
programs, interactive media and merchandise. *National
Geographic* magazine, the Society's official journal,
published in English and 38 local-language editions,
is read by more than 60 million people each month.
The National Geographic Channel reaches 320 million
households in 38 languages in 171 countries. National
Geographic Digital Media receives more than 25 million
visitors a month. National Geographic has funded
more than 10,000 scientific research, conservation
and exploration projects and supports an education
program promoting geography literacy.

For more information, please visit
nationalgeographic.com, call 1-800-NGS LINE
(647-5463), or write to the following address:
National Geographic Society
1145 17th Street N.W.
Washington, D.C. 20036-4688 U.S.A.

Visit us online at nationalgeographic.com/books

For librarians and teachers: ngchildrensbooks.org

More for kids from National Geographic:
kids.nationalgeographic.com

For information about special discounts for bulk
purchases, please contact National Geographic Books
Special Sales: ngspecsales@ngs.org

For rights or permissions inquiries, please contact
National Geographic Books Subsidiary Rights:
ngbookrights@ngs.org

Paperback ISBN: 978-1-4263-1364-6
Reinforced library binding ISBN: 978-1-4263-1365-3

Printed in Hong Kong
13/THK/1